IN THE
NATIONAL INTEREST

General Sir John Monash once exhorted a graduating class to 'equip yourself for life, not solely for your own benefit but for the benefit of the whole community'. At the university established in his name, we repeat this statement to our own graduating classes, to acknowledge how important it is that common or public good flows from education.

Universities spread and build on the knowledge they acquire through scholarship in many ways, well beyond the transmission of this learning through education. It is a necessary part of a university's role to debate its findings, not only with other researchers and scholars, but also with the broader community in which it resides.

Publishing for the benefit of society is an important part of a university's commitment to free intellectual inquiry. A university provides civil space for such inquiry by its scholars, as well as for investigations by public intellectuals and expert practitioners.

This series, In the National Interest, embodies Monash University's mission to extend knowledge and encourage informed debate about matters of great significance to Australia's future.

Professor Margaret Gardner AC
President and Vice-Chancellor,
Monash University

MICHAEL MINTROM

ADVANCING HUMAN RIGHTS

MONASH
UNIVERSITY
PUBLISHING

Monash University Publishing
Matheson Library Annexe
40 Exhibition Walk
Monash University
Clayton, Victoria 3800, Australia
https://publishing.monash.edu

Monash University Publishing brings to the world publications which advance the best traditions of humane and enlightened thought.

ISBN: 9781922633279 (paperback)
ISBN: 9781922633293 (ebook)

Series: In the National Interest
Editor: Louise Adler
Project manager & copyeditor: Paul Smitz
Designer: Peter Long
Typesetter: Cannon Typesetting
Proofreader: Gillian Armitage
Printed in Australia by Ligare Book Printers

A catalogue record for this book is available from the National Library of Australia.

The paper this book is printed on is in accordance with the standards of the Forest Stewardship Council®. The FSC® promotes environmentally responsible, socially beneficial and economically viable management of the world's forests.

For all human rights activists, and those who will be.

May I show an affirming flame.

ADVANCING HUMAN RIGHTS

In the context of COVID-19, there was greater than usual discussion of human rights in Australia. Many people felt seriously constrained by the various lockdowns. Some took to the streets to oppose vaccine mandates. We might say that COVID-19 prompted a flood of debate about people's rights and how well the state protected those rights. More specifically, efforts by governments to protect the lives of those most vulnerable to the virus resulted in the temporary curtailment of freedoms that we typically take for granted. Nobody likes to have their freedoms restricted. And so, government measures were often portrayed as having negative impacts on human rights.

But that is not the whole story, as became clear to me during the pandemic. In 2021, Emilline Law Kwang was completing a Master of Public Policy degree at Monash University. She approached me to supervise her research project, which explored how employees working from home to reduce the spread of COVID-19 created new opportunities for people with disabilities to be included in the labour market. Despite Australia being a signatory to the United Nations (UN) Convention on the Rights of Persons with Disabilities, people in this country with disabilities are twice as likely to be unemployed as people without disabilities. Frequently, employers have concerns about how they will effectively accommodate people with disabilities in their workplaces. The sudden imposition of the government requirement to work from home changed all that.

The emerging evidence was surprising. For a substantial number of people with disabilities, the new norm of working from home made them feel less constrained than before and more able to contribute to the workplace. They did not have to confront, on a daily basis, their differences from others. Furthermore, they often found it easier to participate in paid work because the accommodations in their own homes made it feasible.[1]

Changing norms and expectations can have big implications for social inclusion and, by extension, for the exercising of human rights. If working from home is feasible and productive, why not let more people do it? Too often, we fail to ask questions like this. Reflecting on how the pandemic prompted a shift to performing a job away from the workplace, Joan Williams, a labour lawyer, observed that 'the only thing holding back flexible work arrangements was a failure of imagination'.[2] In turn, this failure of imagination keeps us from advancing human rights. We can, and should, do better.

Because Monash University abided by work-from-home rules during the pandemic, Emilline and I only ever met via Zoom. So I was amazed when I read her LinkedIn post celebrating her graduation. She wrote:

> I was never meant to achieve much … at least that's what doctors predicted. I wasn't supposed to study or exert myself because my body and even my brain might not be able to cope. Cerebral Palsy is one of those illnesses where you can't know how much it will affect your life …

Our Zoom meetings made Emilline's disability invisible to me. We focused on the work to be done, and on approaches to doing it. Emilline achieved a lot of success in her studies at Monash.[3]

As a scholar of public policy, I am interested in how changes in policy design can serve to advance human rights. My broader perspective is that societies and governments should treat public policies as investments. Good investments today generate a positive stream of benefits into the future. When talking about investments, we usually think about money being spent now to generate subsequent financial benefits. That is an important part of the investment approach to policy design. But we also need to recognise that good policy investments can generate many other positive benefits.

Seeking explicitly to advance human rights does not necessarily mean we should radically change how public policies are designed and developed. Indeed, relatively small changes—such as requiring people to work from home during a pandemic—can produce positive consequences, some of which might not have been foreseen. My central purpose here is to show why policy designers should routinely assess how policy changes can support the advancement of human rights, and in doing so have them serve as policy investments that produce benefits for all of society.[4]

THE UNIVERSAL DECLARATION OF HUMAN RIGHTS

The Universal Declaration of Human Rights was adopted by the UN General Assembly in 1948. It set an agenda for actions that governments should take both to protect and advance human rights. The language used throughout the document leaves room for a degree of interpretation around meanings. This suggests that large differences can be observed in the practices of nations towards their populations, even as each nation affirms its support for human rights. Some nations might seek simply to be considered 'beyond reproach' with respect to protecting human rights. Others might aim to continually advance the human rights of individuals and groups. That difference matters.

Philosophy professor Brian Orend suggests the analogy of holding an airline ticket.[5] The ticket entitles you to a flight, and as the holder of the ticket, your primary object is to be on that flight. Extending from Orend, we can point out that people can have very different experiences of a flight—even individuals who are on the same plane. In writing about advancing human rights, my interest lies in seeing that as many people as possible get to experience a good flight. For that to happen, we need to go beyond thinking purely in legal terms about human rights. We need to think hard about the planning of public policies, and how well-designed policies can do much to improve our life experiences. I would go even further and argue that paying special attention to advancing the human rights of particular groups in particular settings can serve to advance the quality of life for all people.

The Nazi atrocities inflicted upon millions of people in Europe during Adolf Hitler's reign as the German Führer provided a compelling motivation for those who championed the Universal Declaration of Human Rights in the wake of World War II. Indeed, understanding this history clarifies much about the language of the document, including its opening statement that 'all human beings are born free and equal in dignity and rights'. The Universal Declaration contains thirty articles enumerating and elaborating on our rights and freedoms.

Of course, concerns about the protection and advancement of human rights have been expressed in various forms for centuries, even during the same period in history. Take the late-eighteenth-century examples of the US Bill of Rights (1791), Thomas Paine's *Rights of Man* (1791) and Mary Wollstonecraft's *A Vindication of the Rights of Woman* (1792). Each was produced in response to different sets of circumstances, and all three prompted much subsequent discussion of human rights.

In the years since the ratification of the Universal Declaration of Human Rights, other conventions and statements have been adopted by groups of nations, by individual nations, and by jurisdictions at the subnational level. Most of these contributions to the advancement of human rights can trace elements of their motivation back to the Universal Declaration. The same can be said for most efforts, through the passage of laws and the creation of government and non-government organisations (NGOs), that have been dedicated to the protection and promotion of human rights since 1948.

As a prosperous, thriving democracy that values multiculturalism, Australia is uniquely positioned to be a beacon to the world when it comes to advancing human rights.[6] We must do all we can to ensure that human rights are not impinged upon by laws, prejudice, or outdated cultural or religious norms. The Australian Human Rights Commission frequently has been the loudest in calling out those cases. Other entities at both the national and state/territory levels likewise have been strong advocates for the protection of human rights. It is now essential that human rights be given a central place in public policy discussions. That is how we can go from the necessary condition of protecting human rights to the even more desirable position of continually advancing human rights for all people—an objective that is entirely consistent with the spirit of the Universal Declaration of Human Rights.

PUBLIC POLICIES AS INVESTMENTS

In treating public policies as investments, careful efforts must be made to determine if the financial gains to society from a specific policy can be expected to exceed the costs of implementing it.[7] The approach warrants careful scrutiny because the normative implications—especially when public policy investments are narrowly construed—can be unpleasant. In a relevant commentary published in *The Guardian Weekly*, Madeleine Bunting noted: 'Caring for others cannot be totted up according to a calculus of costs and returns.' Bunting went on to state:

> Care for children fits into a marketised under-standing of relationships: we talk of 'investing' in our children. The state sees children as important because of their future worth to the economy as labour. But in this marketised mindset, the elderly have no economic value; they are per-ceived as a burden. The only values ascribed to the elderly are found ... in silver-haired celebrities still working ...[8]

Bunting's critique is not of the investment perspective so much as of the narrowness with which people apply it when discussing the policy choices of governments, or the day-to-day choices of citizens. I take the view that good public policy analysis should begin with a consideration of the goals that governments wish to promote. Start with public value. The analysis should then indicate an effective strategy—a model of investment—for increasing the likelihood that public value will be enhanced, rather than inadvertently displaced or ignored. Indeed, an assumption underlying this approach is that the explicit and thorough analysis of government choices is the best way of encouraging society to generate the greatest good for the greatest number of people.

The investment perspective can be applied in a manner that is consistent with the deeply compassionate goal of maximising human wellbeing over the course of individual lives. That is the approach taken in this essay. More specifically, I believe we should be paying much more attention to how public policy choices can serve to advance human rights in society, acknowledging that some of those choices may not produce a financial gain. We need to be explicit about instances where advancing human rights will yield a positive financial return and instances where doing so will not necessarily make sense economically. The more explicit we can be about our policy investments, the more clearly and openly we will be able to discuss trade-offs. In compassionate societies, efforts are always made to protect and support those without the capability to protect and support themselves.

POLICY DESIGN TO ADVANCE HUMAN RIGHTS

What might policy designers do to advance human rights? They must first pay attention. Too often, questions of human rights are not given adequate attention in discussions of public policy and policy design. This work tends to be reactive.[9] When a problem becomes salient, efforts are made to get that problem onto the public agenda and to have elected politicians and their advisors devise ways of addressing it. Given time and financial pressures, the bias is always towards finding *sufficient* solutions to problems. While the costs of policy changes are always considered, and who wins and who loses is usually contemplated, other matters are often pushed to the edge of the discussion. Remarkably, the question of how to most effectively implement policy change can be given short shrift.[10]

Important aspects of public policy proposals can remain unaddressed unless some kind of mandate is put in place to ensure that they will be attended to. For example, the gendered implications of policy design are most likely to be considered when government systems include a ministry, department or agency charged with explicitly viewing policy proposals in that light. Entities established to advance human rights are not necessarily consulted during public policy development, and more should be done to have that happen. At the same time, it would be very helpful if policy designers were to routinely ask questions about the human rights implications of specific proposals during the policy development phase. Given that we habitually consider the financial implications of public policies, it seems entirely reasonable that we should also think about their implications for the advancement of human rights.

Prison release is one area where society would greatly benefit from putting the progression of human rights at the heart of policymaking, not just in financial terms but also in regards to human welfare. The effective management of a prisoner's release can do a lot to promote better social outcomes. Similarly, the school-to-prison pipeline and early childhood education are other areas in which policy changes could advance human rights. Importantly, these policy changes would also represent good investments—there is plenty of evidence to support the claim that reforms in these areas would yield both economic and social gains for our communities.

PRISON RELEASE

One night in mid-October 2021, four-year-old Cleo Smith went missing while holidaying in a tent with her family at Blowholes Campground, midway up the coast of Western Australia. As the days turned into weeks, with no sign of the young girl, many held grave fears for her safety. After an excruciating eighteen days, Western Australian police finally found the girl locked in a room of a small house in the town of Carnarvon, 80 kilometres from where she'd first gone missing. Fortunately, she was alive and well.

Within minutes of rescuing Cleo Smith, the police arrested her alleged abductor, Terence Kelly, placing him in custody. All eyes were on this man, who would ultimately plead guilty to the crime. A few days after his arrest, media coverage showed Kelly in leg-irons and handcuffs, shoeless, being escorted by armed riot squad guards onto a plane for a flight to Perth, where he would be placed in Casuarina Prison, the state's maximum-security correctional facility.

In contemporary society, few people usually witness the operations of prisons, including how prisoners are treated. But media coverage of the arrest and transportation of Terence Kelly was intense because of the nature of the crime and the time it took for police to locate and rescue Cleo Smith. Human rights advocates voiced concern over the wide circulation of the image of an Aboriginal man in chains, surrounded by an all-white group of prison guards. This was countered by the explanation that Kelly was in chains because he had twice needed hospitalisation due to attempting self-harm while being held in Carnarvon.

The safe and orderly functioning of society calls for many rules. Among other things, this means society must establish effective punishments for people who break those rules. Australia is no different from any other country in this regard. But the Universal Declaration of Human Rights has a lot to say about the administration of these rules. Specifically, all of us have 'the right to recognition everywhere as a person before the law'. None of us are to be 'subjected to arbitrary arrest, detention or exile'. And we must also be protected from torture and 'cruel, inhuman or degrading treatment or punishment'.

Observing a prisoner who has just been charged with an egregious crime, what do people feel? Common emotions might include fear, contempt, even hatred. It would appear that few feel sympathy for such a prisoner, or sadness about the complex circumstances that likely contributed to the crime occurring. Yet human rights laws entitle those under arrest to a certain level of protection. Even when convicted, when they are deliberately removed from society, they are to be allowed some dignity, even as they serve time for their crimes.

And what of those who are released back into society? Many people might judge former prisoners as the least deserving people in the community. But that punitive, often unexamined way of thinking can also bring its own problems. Another way to view recently released prisoners is to see them as precarious members of society.

A common pattern of behaviour among released prisoners is that, after a brief 'honeymoon period' back in the community, they revert to committing crime. Recidivism among released prisoners can then lead to serial incarceration. This pattern is consistent with the notion of certain people 'living a life of crime', where they continually bounce between prison and short stints of freedom. The overall result can be devastating for those individuals. It also means that crimes keep being committed, making society less safe and less orderly than we would like it to be. Is there a better way? The answer, based on careful research, appears to be a resounding 'Yes'.

Chris Martin, a researcher at the University of New South Wales, recently conducted a study with some colleagues on the role of housing assistance in supporting released prisoners.[11] The team interviewed relevant actors in and around the criminal justice system. They also made use of a unique dataset combining information from several government sources in New South Wales. Martin notes that, while leaving prison is often referred to as 'going home', currently more than half of people exiting Australian prisons either expect to be homeless or do not know where they will be staying. For some, going into prison will have ended their previous housing arrangement. But, in fact, a third of all people entering prison do so from a situation of homelessness. With more than half of prisoners also having been in prison previously, Martin highlights a vicious, costly cycle of imprisonment and homelessness.

The link between imprisonment and home-lessness is especially acute for people with complex needs. That includes former prisoners who have a mental health condition, a cognitive disability, or both. People with these conditions are over-represented in prison: about 40 per cent of those imprisoned have been diagnosed with a mental health condition, and 33 per cent may have some degree of cognitive impairment. These people can often become enmeshed in years of ongoing interactions with the criminal justice system.

From their interviews, Martin and his col-leagues conclude that the consensus among professionals engaging with the criminal justice system is that insecure, temporary accommo-dation is stressful and diverts ex-prisoners and support agencies from addressing other pressing needs. For example, it makes it harder for those professionals to work with ex-prisoners in ways that will reduce recidivism. Calling on data that tracked ex-prisoners over a period of years, Martin compares outcomes for over 600 former prisoners in public housing and another 600 who did not have access to public housing. The evidence clearly shows that those who were able to secure public housing upon release were significantly less likely to be involved in police incidents and court appearances. They were also much less likely to spend time back in prison. This means reduced costs to the criminal justice system. In their quantitative analysis and via case studies of people who have gone back and forth between society and prison, the researchers showed that significant financial benefits accrue to the community when people can be kept out of prison. The costs associated with placing ex-prisoners in public housing are greatly outweighed by the costs of having them return to prison.

This evidence strongly affirms the argument for greater provision of social housing to people exiting prison, particularly for those with complex support needs. Accommodation could be in the form of public housing or housing provided by community groups, including Indigenous NGOs. Relatively secure, affordable public housing provides an element of stability in the lives of ex-prisoners. This can help them avoid reoffending and also gives them greater capacity to receive and engage with support services.

We currently give too little attention to the actions that could be taken to rehabilitate prisoners so that, upon their release, they are better able to integrate with society and live productive, law-abiding lives. The study noted above suggests people with serious mental health issues can navigate the criminal justice system for some time without any diagnosis occurring. This suggests that insufficient efforts are being made to understand the family and social circumstances of prisoners, and what kinds of non-state support they can expect to receive upon release from prison.

At the time of his arrest, Terence Kelly was thirty-six years old. He lived alone in Carnarvon, in a house owned by Western Australia's Department of Communities. He had no prior convictions. This may suggest that ensuring people have a safe place to call home is no guarantee against them committing crimes. Fair enough, but it is a starting point. Kelly is a troubled man with a complex and difficult family background. Other forms of intervention might have lowered the risk that he would commit a serious crime.

What stands in the way of efforts to support the integration of released prisoners into society is a combination of punitive thinking and a fixation on avoiding more costs being levied on already expensive prisons. But that combination serves to perpetuate the prison–freedom 'bounce' effect, which is ultimately more costly to society than any expenses associated with supporting released prisoners. The argument could be made that former prisoners should not be prioritised for public housing over other, more deserving people who have not committed crimes. But making this housing available to released prisoners is good public policy because it has been shown to reduce the likelihood of released prisoners committing further crimes. In such instances, the provision of public housing supports safe and orderly communities. To the extent that it keeps people out of the justice system and prison, it saves money for society. To the extent that it supports former prisoners to potentially join the paid workforce, it raises the odds that those who previously cost taxpayers a lot of public money to house in prison could go on to become taxpayers themselves.

This is an instance where efforts to advance the human right to housing can also produce broader benefits to society. Investing to ensure public housing for former prisoners might not be popular public policy, but it is public policy in the national interest.

THE SCHOOL-TO-PRISON PIPELINE

In July 2016, a report on ABC TV's *Four Corners* program titled 'Australia's Shame' documented the abuse of juveniles held in the Don Dale Youth Detention Centre in Darwin, and elsewhere. Among the sickening images was footage showing Aboriginal teenager Dylan Voller shirtless, strapped and cuffed to a mechanical restraint chair, his head covered in a spit mask, apparently to protect him from self-harm. So grotesque were the revelations of maltreatment that the Australian human rights commissioner at the time, Gillian Triggs, called for a royal commission to be set up to investigate places like Don Dale. The Royal Commission into the Protection and Detention of Children in the Northern Territory was established within weeks of the *Four Corners* broadcast.

Led by Margaret White and Mick Gooda, the royal commission delivered its report to the Commonwealth and Northern Territory governments in November 2017. To produce it, the commissioners drew upon insights from formal public hearings, interviews, site visits, and the review of many documents. The commissioners concluded that, among other things, youth detention centres were not fit places for accommodating and rehabilitating children and young people. They noted instances of children being subjected to verbal abuse and physical control, including being denied access to basic human needs such as water, food and the use of toilets. Children were also dared or bribed to carry out degrading and humiliating acts, and to commit acts of violence on each other. Youth justice officers restrained children by applying force to their heads, necks and torsos. The isolation of individuals was done inappropriately and punitively, inconsistent with the Northern Territory's *Youth Justice Act*. These practices caused suffering to many children and young people, and it was anticipated that in a number of cases they would result in lasting psychological damage. The commissioners also noted: 'Staff ignored the rules, or did not know the rules and broke the law. Senior people in Government knew about this and did nothing.'[12]

In its findings, the royal commission called for big changes in how children are treated in welfare and detention. It proposed 'a paradigm shift' in youth justice to increase diversion and therapeutic approaches. The other recommendations included placing a greater focus on 'early intervention', where children and young people and their families receive help and support before problems occur with the law.

The *Four Corners* report alleged—and the royal commission confirmed—that extremely vulnerable young people were being systematically abused in youth detention centres in Australia. Had it not been for that investigation and the subsequent reporting, the abuse in the Northern Territory might well have continued unchecked. The royal commission was actioned because the routinised practices of prison guards had become so egregious that they could no longer control the narrative about what had been happening in the youth detention system.

The abuse uncovered by the Royal Commission into the Protection and Detention of Children in the Northern Territory remains cause for outrage. It should never have happened. Turning to the good design of public policy, we now need to consider the series of steps that result in young people landing in detention centres in the first place. What we find in Australia is a pattern that fits what has been termed in the United States 'the school-to-prison pipeline'.[13] From the perspective of advancing human rights, the school-to-prison pipeline is of deep concern for multiple reasons.

Criminologists who write about the school-to-prison pipeline tend to consistently make four claims. First, schools often make insufficient efforts to meet the educational requirements of highly vulnerable children coming to them with special needs or from challenging home situations. Also, as these highly vulnerable children move through the school system, they often find themselves being treated as a problem, which means being excluded from regular classroom environments—for example, in the form of school suspensions. And when these children are suspended from school, they are at greater risk of engaging in unlawful behaviour, which can lead them into contact with the police. Finally, time spent in the youth justice system can lead to ongoing anti-social and unlawful behaviour, which in turn can eventuate in those young people being sentenced to time in prison.

A report produced in 2017 by the Australian Institute of Criminology presents an analysis of data from the International Youth Development Study, a large longitudinal investigation of adolescent development. That analysis strongly suggests the existence of a school-to-prison pipeline in Australia.[14] In addition, recent evidence from the Australian Institute of Health and Welfare (AIHW) documents significantly worse schooling outcomes for Indigenous children compared with non-Indigenous children. Another AIHW report reveals that half of all the young people who were in detention on an average night in the April–June quarter of 2021 were Aboriginal or Torres Strait Islander people. Given that Indigenous Australians make up just 6 per cent of the Australian population aged 10–17, this is a massive level of over-representation in youth detention.[15]

When the NT royal commission called for 'a paradigm shift' and a greater focus on 'early intervention', the commissioners were tacitly acknowledging the reality of a school-to-prison pipeline, which is backed up by recent statistical reports on young people in Australia. This is clear evidence that we are failing many of our children.

More specifically, it is allowing many situations to arise where we could readily question the extent to which Australia is meeting its obligations under the UN Declaration of Human Rights to provide education at 'fundamental stages' to all young people. And, certainly, we must ask to what extent Australia is failing to provide education 'directed to the full development of the human personality'.

An ongoing debate in the field of criminal justice concerns the effectiveness of imprisoning people convicted of crimes, the merits of lengthy sentences, and viable alternatives that both promote public safety and transform those convicted into productive, law-abiding citizens. High incarceration rates in the United States over recent decades have prompted initiatives to reduce the cost to government, as well as the human cost. One of these programs, termed 'justice reinvestment', proposes a two-step process.[16] The first step involves working with offenders to reduce the risk of subsequent reoffending. The second involves using the savings from reduced prison occupancy to strengthen the provision of public services in communities that have historically generated the largest number of offenders.

Clearly, there are enduring issues around how violent criminals might be most effectively managed to promote community safety. Nonetheless, with evidence suggesting that incarceration may not be the most effective way of promoting public safety, justice reinvestment has been touted as advancing 'fiscally sound, data-driven criminal justice policies to break the cycle of recidivism, avert prison expenditures, and make communities safer'.[17] Since 2003, more than half of the US states have participated in some aspect of this initiative. And while individual states may have taken different approaches, all have followed a common strategy. First, analyse the relevant data and develop policy options. Then adopt new policies and put reinvestment strategies in place. Finally, measure the performance of any reinvestment efforts. This involves modelling options and generating evidence to support the development of diversionary programs. The notion of justice reinvestment has now caught on internationally, and efforts are underway to apply it in Australia.[18]

In 2009, former social justice commissioner Tom Calma introduced the justice reinvestment concept here. He suggested it could reduce the over-representation of Indigenous children and adults in the criminal justice system. In Australia, policy decisions that favour imprisonment have a disproportionate impact on Aboriginal and Torres Strait Islander individuals and communities. From an economic perspective, the operations of civil and criminal justice systems incur significant cost. In addition, increased incarceration rates rarely have much, if any, effect on crime rates. Evidence around the world has demonstrated that there is no clear link between crime rates and incarceration.[19] Instead of relying on overly punitive policies, justice reinvestment seeks to understand the drivers of crime and apply interventions accordingly. In other words, those associated with the movement have been working to disrupt the school-to-prison pipeline.

The town of Bourke in New South Wales has been applying the justice reinvestment model for a decade now.[20] Bourke is one of the most disadvantaged localities in Australia. The majority of crimes committed by young people there tend to be driving offences, property offences and breaches of bail. Aboriginal people make up a small proportion of the general population, but Aboriginal youth often comprise half those in juvenile detention. And this has come at a huge cost.[21]

Discussing the situation, Alistair Ferguson, a leader of the local justice reinvestment project, has said:

Kids were being taken away. Too many of my community were being locked up. Families were being shattered, again and again … And this was happening despite the huge amount of money government was channelling through a large number of service organisations in this town. So we started talking together. We decided that a new way of thinking and doing things needed to be developed that helped our children. We decided it was time for our community to move beyond the existing service delivery model … which had clearly failed.[22]

In 2012, the Bourke Aboriginal Community Working Party in partnership with Just Reinvest NSW produced their justice reinvestment strategy. It aimed to provide better-coordinated support to vulnerable Aboriginal children and families. The first stage of the project focused on building trust between the residents and service providers, identifying community priorities, and collecting data on the drivers of crime. The strategy was to quantify the costs of imprisoning people and then estimate the savings associated with potential policy changes. The project has taken a localised approach to public safety that targets money for intervention programs in health, education, job creation and job training in 'high risk' sectors. While the trial is ongoing, it has already shown that such efforts can increase community safety while reducing offending and avoiding an over-reliance on imprisonment, including youth detention.

The school-to-prison pipeline is devastating for many of society's most vulnerable young people. It can divert children from gaining the education they need and channel them into lives of crime and incarceration. The costs to the individual are high. The costs to society are high, too. The justice reinvestment movement represents a change in approach that can help turn vulnerable lives around and at the same time save society money. At its best, it takes people who might have spent their lives being a burden to the taxpayer and transforms them into well-integrated people who contribute to society in many ways.

That positive result helps us steer clear of the danger that vulnerable people will have their human rights violated. Indeed, efforts to break the school-to-prison pipeline are consistent with the advancement of human rights. Public policy focused on this goal would progress us a long way from 'Australia's Shame' over vulnerable young people being brutalised in youth detention centres and initiated into lives of crime.

EARLY CHILDHOOD EDUCATION

As mentioned earlier, the Royal Commission into the Protection and Detention of Children in the Northern Territory recommended in its final report that, among other things, greater emphasis be placed on 'early intervention'. That recommendation is consistent with evidence from an array of studies dating back decades. The research highlights the significant and sustained value to individuals, and to society as a whole, of ensuring children have access to high-quality early childhood education, prior to entering primary school. More importantly, the benefits of a child's participation in this accrue in the greatest measure to those coming from families with less-educated parents and lower household incomes. It is vital to note the emphasis on 'high-quality' education here—the same gains are not observed when children participate in services that have a minimal focus on wellbeing, structured play and cognitive development.

The relevant evidence has been generated by longitudinal studies, mostly conducted in the United States, that track individuals over many years.[23] Those who attend high-quality early childhood education services have been found to perform better at school, stay longer in school, attend tertiary institutions, obtain and remain in steady employment, avoid criminal behaviour, get married and stay married, and form families. They are also found to experience better physical and mental health later in their lives.[24] These are significant benefits for the individual. And financially speaking, the gains to society are considerable, too. This led economist James Heckman to conclude: 'Early childhood development is perhaps the strongest investment we could make on a raw return-on-investment basis.'[25]

From a human rights perspective, we might say that universal access to high-quality education early in life is a powerful means of advancing the human rights of many citizens. Due to receiving this educational boost, they are more likely to be able to experience freedoms and opportunities throughout their lives. In the process, they are less likely to engage in actions that impose on the freedoms and opportunities of others. More positively, we might say that they contribute to the advancement of the good society, bringing more to the collective table than they take from it.

What is it about early childhood education that appears to be so vital for setting individuals on a positive trajectory, educationally and in other ways? Various answers have been offered. At the level of the individual child, the evidence suggests that children learn more through these early experiences about how to get along well with others and how to regulate their behaviour and their emotions. This sets them up for transitioning into the more formal learning settings found in primary school. Since the students are less likely to fall behind in their learning, this then reduces the likelihood of them engaging in disruptive classroom activities. It is certainly much more cost-effective and beneficial to invest in early education than in later remedial interventions targeted at poor literacy, school dropouts, and adults with limited basic skills. Beyond this, some studies have noted how the content of early childhood education activities can serve to shape personalities in positive ways, including curriculum content that develops an appreciation in young children of their own rights, and also how they can show respect for the human rights of those around them.[26]

Another body of evidence has noted that contact between children and their families and early childhood educational services allows professionals to more readily identify developmental, social or family-related problems. Those professionals can then arrange suitable additional support where necessary. It is also the case that socialisation opportunities for children and parents reduce the risk of social isolation, which can lead to a range of problems going undetected or undiagnosed; for example, a child with a health problem may receive the appropriate attention much earlier than would otherwise be the case.

There are wellbeing benefits for parents, too. For example, gaining some regular time apart from young children can be a big positive for primary caregivers, especially in terms of their mental health. In addition, placing young children in early childhood education services can allow parents to remain in touch with the labour market or continue their training. There are obvious positive flow-on effects for careers and for household income, and overall, greater resources are clearly beneficial for all members of the household.

It is interesting to note that access to early childhood education is not explicitly stated as a human right in the Universal Declaration, nor in the later UN Convention on the Rights of the Child, which was ratified in 1989. However, there is language in both documents that is certainly consistent with the provision of such education. With the strong evidence we now have concerning the ongoing benefits of participation, it seems reasonable to claim that efforts to increase the proportion of children doing so also serve to advance human rights.[27]

So where is Australia in respect to this? Since 2008, the Australian Government has provided funding to assist states and territories to increase preschool participation through the National Partnership Agreement on Universal Access to Early Childhood Education. The initiative aims to provide universal access to quality preschool programs for all children in the year preceding full-time schooling, for up to 600 hours per annum. This translates into fifteen hours a week for forty weeks of the year.[28] If managed by a preschool, itself operated either by government or non-government entities, the program can be delivered from a standalone facility, or the pre-school may be integrated or co-located within a bigger school. Alternatively, centre-based daycare services, which look after children aged 0–5, may offer a preschool program run by a qualified teacher. As with preschools, centre-based day care can be offered from a separate facility or be located within a school, and it can be managed by for-profit or not-for-profit organisations.

In recent times, calls have been made for the increased resourcing of early childhood education in Australia.[29] The aim is to reach more children in the year before they attend school, as well as more three-year-olds. A widely held view among educators is that children could benefit from exposure to high-quality early childhood education for at least two years prior to entering primary school. Investment in this can only be good for children, families and the nation. It can also generate powerful results in terms of advancing human rights. The challenge for Australia is to increase access to such services for the families who are currently the most marginalised. These people are often of Aboriginal and Torres Strait Islander heritage. Those who have recently experienced migration to Australia are also at risk of social exclusion.

INVESTING TO ADVANCE
HUMAN RIGHTS

The American civil rights activist Rosa Parks famously observed: 'I believe we are here on earth to live, grow, and do what we can to make this world a better place for all people to enjoy freedom.'[30] This suggests there is always more that we can do to improve the human rights and freedoms many avail themselves of. The foregoing discussions of prison release, the school-to-prison pipeline and early childhood education have each highlighted how policy changes can advance human rights while also yielding financial gains for society. In all three cases, appropriate policy changes could generate cost savings and tax revenues in the future that would more than compensate for the initial investments.

Those findings refer to broad populations, not to individuals. We cannot say that every ex-prisoner placed in public housing will not reoffend.

We cannot say that keeping troubled teenagers in school will necessarily keep them from committing crime. And we cannot say that high-quality early childhood education will ensure that all who experience it will have better life chances than if they had not. But we can say, with a high degree of confidence, that policies intended to promote better outcomes in these examples typically will do so. Given this, we can then ask: how might investing to advance human rights become a more common feature of policy development?

The challenge here has two parts. First, identify ways in which public policies can advance human rights. And second, test the likelihood that appropriate policy changes can serve as investments—that is, test how a policy change might generate a stream of benefits over time that will be greater than the costs associated with providing the relevant supports or services. It's worth emphasising that this second challenge is just as important to address as the first.

It provides clear economic reasoning for supporting a policy change. This means justifications for
policy changes can be made without even having
to invoke human rights. In an essay on advancing
human rights, that last comment must seem odd.
But there is a logic to this, which I will further
explain below.

Much could be done to advance human rights
if policy designers routinely follow several steps
when thinking about these rights. The first is
to select a specific context in which it's believed
that human rights could be advanced. Next,
assemble evidence of the factors currently con-
straining human rights in that context. Develop
a process-tracing method to show how current,
specific institutional arrangements, social practices or decision-making result in less-than-ideal
outcomes from a human rights perspective.
Then propose policy changes to advance human
rights in this setting, accompanied by an estimate
of the associated costs and benefits. Finally,

address concerns about the potential negative consequences of the suggested changes.

In 2021, the Royal Commission into Aged Care Quality and Safety delivered its final report. Based on its findings, we could readily conclude that more needs to be done in aged-care facilities in Australia to protect and advance the human rights of residents. Among other things, the royal commission found that people in aged care typically have limited access to services offered by allied health professionals, such as dietitians, exercise physiologists, mental health workers, occupational therapists, speech pathologists, and specialist oral and dental health professionals.[31] Article 25 of the Universal Declaration of Human Rights states:

> Everyone has the right to a standard of living adequate for the health and well-being of himself and of his family, including food, clothing, housing and medical care and necessary social

services, and the right to security in the event of … [among other things] old age …[32]

On reading the royal commission report, it is evident that the human rights of elderly people in Australia could be advanced by increasing access to allied health professionals.

Evidence is always needed to make a strong claim that a problem exists. Even then, we need to make a convincing argument that solutions are available to effectively address the problem. Referring to what witnesses had described, the Royal Commission into Aged Care Quality and Safety noted the crucial role of allied health in maintaining mobility and functionality, and in providing restorative care in response to acute events. It then emphasised that many people receiving aged-care services do not have sufficient access to such crucial services.

The royal commission noted the importance of an individual's reablement and rehabilitation after having spent time in hospital due to injury or the need for surgery. Reablement involves taking a planned approach to community care and services for the elderly. It is intended to help a person re-establish their daily living skills and their connections to the community. Such activities, when successfully executed, allow people to become rehabilitated and experience life in ways approximating what they experienced before entering hospital. The royal commission recommended that

> care at home should include the allied health care that an older person needs to restore their physical and mental health to the highest level possible—and to maintain it at that level for as long as possible—to maximise their independence and autonomy.[33]

The royal commission went on to assert that greater access to allied care would promote the 'independence and autonomy' of elderly people, prolonging their time in their own homes and in the community before they enter aged-care residences. It seems reasonable to suggest that any efforts towards these goals also serve to advance the human rights of elderly people.

This example nicely illustrates a couple of points of importance to the broader discussion in this essay. To begin with, it seems entirely plausible that carefully targeted improvements in access to allied health services could help elderly people to live in their own homes for longer than if such improvements were not made. It is also plausible that the benefits could outweigh the costs. In this case, the major monetary benefit to consider is the savings realised by the government when elderly people do not have to be placed in aged-care residences. For policy analysts and advocates, the need to forcefully make the human rights case for increasing access to allied health services can be greatly reduced when the basic economics of the situation point to positive gains by society.

Increasing funding for allied health services for Australia's elderly makes a lot of sense, so long as those extra funds are directed to where the needs are most acute. Governments always face funding constraints. This means that careful decisions need to be made about prioritising where funds are spent. Potentially, there are ways of funding the additional delivery of these services that would generate extra benefits that outweigh any extra costs, but this cannot be guaranteed. In the best-case scenario, more funding would advance the human rights of many elderly people by keeping them healthy, independent, and in the community for longer. The less-desirable scenario is that more funding would assist a few elderly people, while leaving many others no better off than under the present arrangements.

When we consider ways in which to advance human rights in Australia, many other candidates for policy change come to mind. While egregious cases of human rights abuse are rare, there are various instances where much could be done to progress these rights.[34] Placing an explicit focus on advancing human rights holds the promise of also creating and shaping better public policies. Two candidates for policy change, following the framework described here, are the provision of health care to Indigenous peoples, and the issue of discrimination against LGBTQIA+ people, particularly the young.

ADDRESSING INADEQUATE PRIMARY HEALTHCARE SERVICES FOR INDIGENOUS PEOPLE

Poor health outcomes for Indigenous people are both tragic and expensive. Since 2006, Aboriginal and Torres Strait Islander Health Performance Framework reports have provided information about the key drivers of Indigenous health and the overall performance of the health system. These reports have highlighted the continuing health inequalities between Indigenous and non-Indigenous Australians. They have also noted broader social inequalities in areas that can affect health, such as housing, education, employment, and access to adequate health care.[35]

In 2015–17, life expectancy at birth was 71.6 years for Indigenous males and 75.6 years for Indigenous females. The gap between Indigenous and non-Indigenous Australians was 8.6 years for males and 7.8 years for females. Healthcare professionals talk of 'disease burden', which refers to the impact of living with illness and injury and dying prematurely—the rate of disease burden among Aboriginal and Torres Strait Islander people is estimated at more than double that of non-Indigenous Australians. This means that Indigenous Australians, individually and as a group, lose more years of their lives to health concerns than do non-Indigenous Australians.

Health expenditures reflect the relative need for healthcare services among population groups. In 2015–16, the average hospital spending per person in Australia was $4436 per year for Indigenous people and $2718 for non-Indigenous people. Per-person spending on community health services was $998 per year for the former and $331 for the latter.

The Universal Declaration of Human Rights emphasises that everyone has the right to a standard of living adequate for the health and wellbeing of themselves and their children. But clearly there are long-term, ongoing problems with the health of Aboriginal and Torres Strait Islander people in Australia. Specifically, there is a need for the delivery of culturally safe and respectful primary healthcare services for Australia's Indigenous population. Services that strive to offer cultural safety create environments that allow people to feel spiritually, socially and emotionally safe, as well as physically safe.

In such environments, people feel confident that they will not be assaulted or challenged. They feel that their identity is being embraced, that there is no denial of their identity, of who they are and what they need.[36]

Primary health care is delivered in community settings, such as general practices, community health centres, Aboriginal health services, and allied health practices like physiotherapy. It is usually people's first point of contact with the health system, and the gateway to specialised services. To provide effective health care, services must be accessible, responsive, and culturally safe and respectful. Yet many Aboriginal and Torres Strait Islander people currently face barriers to accessing the health services they need.

The Australian Government provides funding to organisations to provide culturally appropriate primary healthcare services to Aboriginal and Torres Strait Islander people. But although four in five Indigenous Australians live in major cities and regional areas where mainstream health services are typically located, these services are not always accessible to them. The count of potentially preventable hospitalisations offers a useful indicator of current system problems. These are hospital admissions that could have been avoided through preventative measures, like vaccination, or through timely and effective diagnosis and treatment outside the hospital setting. It's thought that, from July 2015 to June 2017, 81 100 hospitalisations of Aboriginal and Torres Strait Islander people were potentially preventable. This is an age-standardised rate of sixty-nine preventable hospitalisations per 1000 Indigenous Australians, compared with twenty-six per 1000 among non-Indigenous Australians. And this rate has only increased in recent years. Evidence from hospital records also shows that, while Aboriginal and Torres Strait Islander people are more likely to be hospitalised than non-Indigenous Australians, they are less likely to receive a medical or surgical procedure while in hospital. Over the same two-year period referenced above, 64 per cent of hospitalisations of Indigenous Australians had a medical or surgical procedure recorded, compared with 81 per cent for non-Indigenous Australians.[37]

While the determinants of population health are complex, it can be deduced from this evidence that there is considerable room for improvement in the delivery of primary healthcare services to Australia's Indigenous population. The challenge is to ensure that Aboriginal and Torres Strait Islander people can get the care and advice they require in a timely fashion. It is a challenge that should be met, as knowledge exists in the community concerning how to do this well.[38] The rate of hospitalisation of Australia's Indigenous population is especially concerning, and the incidence of preventable cases points to clear gaps in the current system. Given that hospital care represents the most costly form of engagement that anyone can have with the healthcare system, anything that reduces the incidence of this will produce cost savings. Beyond that, a greater focus on the delivery of culturally safe and respectful primary care is likely to allow more Aboriginal and Torres Strait Islander people to live healthier and longer lives. In this sense, such care is enabling. It would allow many people in Australia to lead more socially engaged lives than is the case at present.

ADDRESSING DISCRIMINATION AGAINST LGBTQIA+ YOUNG PEOPLE

There was considerable public celebration in 2017 when the Australian Parliament adopted a marriage equality law allowing two people to marry regardless of sex. Australia became the twenty-sixth country in the world to do so, which it did soon after the results were announced of an unprecedented national postal survey where citizens could register their support or otherwise for such a law. Of the voters who participated, 61.6 per cent approved of a law change to allow couples of the same sex to marry. The adoption of this law served to advance human rights in Australia.[39] But commentators have noted that Australia still has a long way to go in recognising and actively defending the human rights of sexual minorities—people who identify with the category LGBTQIA+ (lesbian, gay, bisexual, transgender, queer, intersex and asexual, with the plus sign representing other sexual identities such as gender fluid).[40]

Consider the case of thirteen-year-old Tyrone Unsworth. Tyrone's favourite saying was 'Sticks and stones may break my bones but words will never hurt me'. But words can hurt. Continuous name-calling and bullying can have tragic consequences. In November 2016, while he was a Year 7 student, Tyrone killed himself. His mother attributed his death to the bullying he had endured while at school. These are her words:

> Tyrone ended up being gay and a lot of people started picking on him. He was a really feminine male, he loved fashion, he loved make-up and the boys always picked on him, calling him gay-boy, faggot, fairy; it was a constant thing from Year 5. I feel like these people who were bullying Tyrone are the cause of why he is not here anymore. They pushed him to the edge.[41]

Taking greater steps in schools to address bullying would do much to advance the human rights of LGBTQIA+ people in Australia. It would save precious lives. It would allow more people to fully engage with society and truly flourish. Bullying can be direct in nature, where victims are subject to threats, name-calling, ridicule and physical harm. Bullying can also be relational, where victims are ignored, being deliberately left out of get-togethers, parties, trips and groups, or they have nasty lies, rumours or stories told about them. Bullying can also take place in cyberspace, where victims are subject to upsetting or harmful messages shared by text or on social media platforms.[42] Evidence from Australia and elsewhere indicates that children and young people attending schools who identify as LGBTQIA+ frequently experience bullying.[43]

The literature on bullying in schools contains findings from studies that control for pre-existing health conditions, family situations, and other exposures to violence (such as family violence). Researchers have used such studies to investigate both the immediate and longer-term effects of bullying, confirming that children who are victims of bullying have been consistently found to be at higher risk of anxiety disorder and depression in young adulthood and middle adulthood (18–50 years of age). Furthermore, victims have been found to be at increased risk of displaying psychotic experiences at age eighteen as well as suicidal ideation, attempts and completed suicides. They have also been reported as having poor general health, including more bodily pain and headaches, and slower recovery from illnesses. Moreover, victimised children have been found to have lower educational qualifications, be worse at financial management, and to earn less than their peers throughout their adult lives. They have more trouble making and keeping friends, and are less likely to live with a partner and have social support.[44]

Drawing from a recent national study of Australian high-school students who identify as gender and sexuality diverse, Jacqueline Ullman of the University of Western Sydney reported that participants overwhelmingly depicted a secondary schooling environment in which homophobic language was a regular occurrence and where school staff did not respond with consistency.[45] Almost all of those involved had heard homophobic language at school, with

37 per cent of these young people being subjected to this language daily. Of those who reported classmates using this language within earshot of school staff, just 6 per cent said that these adults always intervened to put a stop to its use. The research also found that transphobic language was commonplace and that teachers rarely intervened to address it. Although less commonly reported, 29 per cent of participants indicated that they had witnessed the school-based physical harassment of classmates who were perceived to be gender and sexuality diverse—7 per cent witnessed such harassment on a weekly basis. Only 11 per cent of young people who witnessed physical harassment which occurred within view of school staff reported that these adults always intervened.

The students subjected to the homophobic and transphobic language, and to physical harassment, reported feeling less connected to school, less confident that their teachers were able to manage bullying and keep them safe, and less assured that their teachers were personally invested in them and in their academic success. These relationships were even more pronounced where students described less-frequent positive intervention by teachers during instances of verbal and physical homophobia and transphobia.

Several self-report measures of academic outcomes were used to examine the relationships between participants' sense of their own academic abilities and their wellbeing at school and the school's climate.[46] Participants who described a more positive schooling environment, where they felt more personally connected to school and cared for by their teachers, had stronger academic outcomes. Those outcomes included higher academic self-concept, greater intentions to attend university, and fewer reported incidences of truancy. Taken together, these findings highlight the link between school climate, wellbeing, and academic outcomes and behaviours for gender and sexuality diverse students.

Researchers who have studied bullying in schools have noted various proven strategies that can help fashion a school culture that promotes respect, recognition, learning, safety and positive experiences for all students.[47] These include reaching out to victims, setting and enforcing clear rules and consequences for bullying behaviours, and supervising students during breaks—especially on playgrounds, in toilet facilities and in busy hallways. Other strategies are having class discussions and activities related to bullying, so that students who might otherwise watch passively become empowered to intervene, and victims are allowed to have a voice free of shame; encouraging active participation by parents and other adults; and framing bullying as a community issue that needs to be addressed by community action.

Based on these indications, it is clear that Australian children and young people identifying as LGBTQIA+ are frequently subjected to bullying behaviours in school. Ongoing exposure to such bullying can have significant long-term negative consequences for an individual's mental health, their educational performance and subsequent workforce participation. It is also important to note that many adults who identify as LGBTQIA+ also face challenges in the workplace, which often result from behaviours similar to those of schoolyard bullies.[48] All of this is deeply concerning. But research also indicates effective steps that can reduce bullying and forge school cultures that are welcoming of all children and young people, regardless of their sexual orientation. There is also evidence to suggest that a strong majority of parents of school-age children support teaching about gender and sexuality diversity in Australian schools.[49]

No formal evidence currently exists concerning the costs and benefits associated with seeking to change the culture of schools to reduce—but preferably eliminate—the bullying of LGBTQIA+ students. But it is obvious that efforts along these lines, supported by appropriate public policy changes, would be highly beneficial to Australian society. Tyrone Unsworth's suicide at age thirteen was an awful but avoidable tragedy. Had Tyrone attended a school offering a safe, supportive environment, he would not have been subjected to the constant bullying that pushed him to the edge. No young person should be subjected to such treatment.

Everyone benefits when young people grow into adults who feel confident enough in themselves to fully participate in society and flourish throughout life. That is why the question of how to advance human rights should lie at the heart of policymaking. Among other things, placing an emphasis on advancing human rights would drive efforts to systematically and effectively address bullying in schools.

LOOKING AHEAD

The Universal Declaration of Human Rights was developed as 'a common standard' to be recognised and observed by all peoples and all nations. The articles in the declaration put the individual at centrestage, emphasising what must be done to ensure that every person can live a free and dignified life. Governments around the world, to differing degrees, have established legal provisions and public policies to protect and promote the human rights of citizens. Australia is no exception, with relevant laws that have been promulgated at the national, state and territory levels. Experts and close observers of human rights in Australia generally take the view that governments here have made good-faith efforts to act consistently with the provisions of the Universal Declaration.

But there is always room for governments to do more to advance human rights. In this essay,

I have focused on the intersection of policy design and advancing human rights. The argument is basic: advancing human rights should be a central focus in all policy design work—it should always receive careful consideration. For human rights to be advanced, governments must continuously act to ensure their policy settings support that outcome. But while the free and dignified life of the individual is fundamental to this, it is also vital to emphasise that advancing human rights for each person has a positive, transformative impact on society as a whole.

Consider the examples discussed earlier, thinking through the life course. Given what we know about the benefits of early intervention, large gains would come to society if we could do more to provide high-quality early childhood education to all children, and especially to those from marginalised backgrounds. We would have a better society if young people struggling in school and at risk of being disruptive could receive the support and services they need before problems get out of hand.

We would also have a better society if children and young people in school could be protected from bullying. We know that LGBTQIA+ young people in particular are frequently subjected to harassment, and that this affects them at school. We also know that they face discrimination in the workplace and in society more broadly. There are ways of addressing these issues. Taking active steps to support LGBTQIA+ young people would allow more members of society to flourish and contribute strongly throughout their lives.

Helping people to live healthy lives is also critical to individual wellbeing, and to a person's capacity to contribute to the lives of those around them. We know there is a significant gap in health outcomes between Indigenous and non-Indigenous Australians. Ensuring that primary healthcare services are culturally appropriate and safe would assist in closing that gap, which would see Indigenous Australians live longer, healthier lives. All of Australian society would benefit.

The same is true for promoting the health of the elderly. Making greater efforts to ensure old people get the allied health supports they need in a timely fashion would allow more of the elderly to live independently in their own homes, or with family members, for longer. The demand for places in aged-care homes would be reduced.

These are just a few examples of situations where changes in public policies would serve to advance the human rights of individuals. Such changes would also generate significant benefits for society as a whole. The fact is that the wellbeing of others enhances our own wellbeing.

A common objection when we talk about positive policy changes is that they will be too expensive—we cannot afford them. But that is not true of the cases discussed here. In an ideal world, the calculus of costs and benefits should not impinge at all on efforts to advance human rights, but we do need to be realists. Financially, the suggested policy changes in all of these areas would generate savings and revenues that outweigh their costs. The advancement of human rights is an investment.

This all raises an obvious question: if there are so many instances where efforts to advance human rights for specific groups would generate benefits for society as a whole, why hasn't this happened already? It hasn't for two main reasons. First, the people who would most benefit from efforts to advance human rights are subjected to pressures that tend to marginalise them in Australian society. And second, Australian politics and policymaking tends to be dominated by elites who have benefited from experiencing the best conditions Australia has to offer—when you live in safe, productive, supportive enclaves, you can easily become insensitive to the challenges faced by others.

But change is possible. It just requires a willingness on the part of political elites to drive it, and to make the arguments to the broader public about why that change is necessary. Advocates for change might be bolstered by the words of Martin Luther King, Jr.: 'The arc of the moral universe is long, but it bends toward justice.'

Australian society would greatly benefit from focusing its attention on advancing human rights. This means that policy designers should put the advancement of human rights at the centre of their work. And whenever policy changes are being considered, analysts and advisors should routinely explore the implications of those changes for human rights.

Here, I have proposed a process for investing in human rights. Fundamentally, this process involves using evidence to guide our understanding of the factors that currently constrain human rights. That careful engagement with evidence then becomes our starting point for establishing how policy changes can serve to advance human rights.

ACKNOWLEDGEMENTS

I have long understood that governments, through their policy choices, can have a profound influence on the life chances of individuals and whole communities. My interest in advancing human rights through public policy has been continuous throughout my career, which began when I worked on social policy issues as an economic analyst in the New Zealand Treasury.

The first time I explicitly connected an investment perspective on policy design with an interest in promoting human flourishing occurred in 2011, when I led a taskforce on early childhood education for the New Zealand

Government. The legacy of that work, which produced *An Agenda for Amazing Children*, is apparent in this essay, where I write of the crucial value to individuals and society of high-quality early childhood education and other forms of early intervention. Following that taskforce work, I started an extensive project of evidence gathering, which led to my book *Public Policy: Investing for a Better World*, published by Oxford University Press in 2019. That book contains eight explorations of connections between treating public policies as investments and activities to promote human rights, using case studies that draw on evidence from the United States. For some years now, I have been keen to tighten my argument and present it with reference to Australian examples. This essay is my first full excursion in pursuit of that goal.

As the foregoing chronology suggests, I have benefited enormously over the years from a diversity of intellectual engagements and policy-focused discussions with many, many people. I mention here those who I have most closely engaged with while completing this essay. I wish to thank Kevin Bell, Professor of Practice and former director of the Castan Centre for Human Rights Law at Monash University, for his inspiration and advice during the planning stages. Kevin and I talked at length about how the perspective that views public policies as investments could be joined with a focus on advancing human rights. Ruby O'Connor provided extensive support as a research assistant. She also discussed how to approach the topic and provided extensive comments on the initial draft.

Jacqui True, Professor of International Relations and Director of the Centre for Gender, Peace and Security at Monash University, gave me considerable guidance on key contributions to the human rights literature. Jacqui and I have previously collaborated on projects relating to the advancement of human rights, including on the pursuit of equal employment opportunities, enhancing the representation of women in leadership roles, and the elimination of violence against women. I appreciate her advice on the orientation of this essay and my choice of cases.

I also extend my deep appreciation to Louise Adler, the series editor, who encouraged me to contribute and showed great patience as I refined the focus of the work and pushed out the date for completion of the manuscript. Thanks also to Paul Smitz, the series coordinator and copyeditor, for his terrific advice and enthusiasm for the project at every step of the production process.

NOTES

1   The trend across many professional areas of working from home has been increasing over the past decade. The pandemic hastened that trend. For relevant discussions see: M Ketchell, 'Coronavirus Could Revolutionize Work Opportunities for People with Disabilities', *The Conversation*, 5 May 2020; and LA Schur, M Ameri and D Kruse, 'Telework after COVID: A "Silver Lining" for Workers with Disabilities?' *Journal of Occupational Rehabilitation*, vol. 30, no. 4, 2020, pp. 521–36.

2   Joan Williams is quoted in Emma Goldberg, 'A Two-Year, 50-Million-Person Experiment in Changing How We Work', *The New York Times*, 14 March 2022.

3   I am grateful to Emilline Law Kwang for allowing me to write about her here, and for drawing my attention to the challenges faced by people with disabilities as they engage with the paid workforce. The policy

of working from home created new opportunities for people with disabilities to participate. Of course, working from home is not ideal in all circumstances. But the pandemic reminded us that flexible thinking and adaptability can allow us to push ahead in difficult times. Sometimes when we do that, we come to appreciate opportunities that we had not seriously considered before.

4   The following four works provide useful overviews of the theory and practice of human rights: Andrew Clapham, *Human Rights: A Very Short Introduction*, Oxford University Press, Oxford, 2007; Jack Donnelly, *Universal Human Rights in Theory and Practice*, 3rd edn, Cornell University Press, Ithaca, NY, 2013; Michael Freeman, *Human Rights*, 2nd edn, Polity Press, Cambridge, 2011; and Michael Goodhart, *Human Rights: Politics and Practice*, Oxford University Press, Oxford, 2009.

5   Brian Orend, *Human Rights: Concept and Context*, Broadview Press, Peterborough, Ontario, 2002, pp. 28–9.

6   For an excellent discussion of human rights in the Australian context, see Louise Chappell, John Chesterman and Lisa Hill, *The Politics of Human Rights in Australia*, Cambridge University Press, Melbourne, 2009. For a discussion of areas where Australia could strengthen its commitment to human rights, see Carolien van Ham, Lisa Hill and Louise Chappell,

'Ten Things Australia Can Do to Be a Human Rights Hero', *The Conversation*, 6 December 2017.

7   For elaboration on the investment perspective on public policy, see Michael Mintrom, *Public Policy: Investing for a Better World*, Oxford University Press, New York, 2019. A shorter treatment can be found in Michael Mintrom and Joannah Luetjens, 'The Investment Approach to Public Service Provision', *Australian Journal of Public Administration*, vol. 77, no. 1, 2018, pp. 136–44.

8   Madeline Bunting, 'Market Has No Use for the Elderly', *The Guardian Weekly*, 28 October 2011, p. 28.

9   This is often because of crowded political agendas and limits to how much attention any issue can be expected to receive: see Bryan D Jones and Frank R Baumgartner, *The Politics of Attention: How Government Prioritizes Problems*, University of Chicago Press, Chicago, 2005.

10 For the classic discussion of this, see Jeffrey L Pressman and Aaron Wildavsky, *Implementation*, University of California Press, Berkeley, 1973. For examples of how implementation problems have been effectively overcome, see Joannah Luetjens, Michael Mintrom and Paul 't Hart (eds), *Successful Public Policy: Lessons from Australia and New Zealand*, ANU Press, Canberra, 2019.

11 Chris Martin, Rebecca Reeve, Ruth McCausland, Eileen Baldry, Pat Burton and Rob White, *Exiting Prison with Complex Support Needs: The Role of*

Housing Assistance, Australian Housing and Urban Research Institute final report no. 361, AHURI, Melbourne, 2021, https://www.ahuri.edu.au/research/final-reports/361 (viewed April 2022).

12 Royal Commission into the Protection and Detention of Children in the Northern Territory, *Report Overview*, 2017, p. 5. Other quotes from the royal commission used in this essay also come from this overview document.

13 For a useful overview, see Kelly Welch, 'School-to-Prison Pipeline', in Christopher J Schreck (ed.), *The Encyclopedia of Juvenile Delinquency and Justice*, John Wiley & Sons, Hoboken, NJ, 2017, pp. 1–5.

14 Sheryl A Hemphill, David J Broderick and Jessica A Heerde, 'Positive Associations between School Suspension and Student Problem Behaviour: Recent Australian Findings', *Trends & Issues in Crime and Criminal Justice*, no. 531, Australian Institute of Criminology, Canberra, June 2017.

15 Australian Institute of Health and Welfare, 'Indigenous Education and Skills: Snapshot', AIHW, Canberra, 16 September 2021; and Australian Institute of Health and Welfare, 'Youth Detention Population in Australia 2021', cat. no. JUV 136, AIHW, Canberra, 2021.

16 See Susan B Tucker and Eric Cadora, 'Justice Reinvestment: To Invest in Public Safety by Reallocating Justice Dollars to Refinance Education, Housing, Healthcare and Jobs', *Ideas for an Open Society*, vol. 3, no. 3, 2003, pp. 2–5.

17 Council of State Governments Justice Center, *Lessons from the States: Reducing Recidivism and Curbing Corrections Costs through Justice Reinvestment*, Council of State Governments, Washington, DC, 2013.

18 See David Brown, Chris Cunneen, Melanie Schwartz, Julie Stubbs and Courtney Young, *Justice Reinvestment: Winding Back Imprisonment*, Palgrave Macmillan, London, 2016.

19 See Michael H Tonry (ed.), *Why Crime Rates Fall and Why They Don't*, University of Chicago Press, Chicago, 2015; Jeremy Travis, Bruce Western and F Stevens Redburn, *The Growth of Incarceration in the United States: Exploring Causes and Consequences*, National Research Council on Law and Justice, National Academies Press, Washington, DC, 2014.

20 For background on Bourke's justice reinvestment initiatives, see Just Reinvest NSW, 'Justice Reinvestment in Bourke', 2022, https://www.justreinvest.org.au/justice-reinvestment-in-bourke (viewed April 2022).

21 The estimated annual cost of incarcerating young Aboriginal people from Bourke is more than $230 000 per person: see Liz Forsyth, Penny Armitage and Ruth Lawrence, *Unlocking the Future: Maranguka Justice Reinvestment in Bourke*, KPMG International, Sydney, 2016; and KPMG, *Maranguka Justice Reinvestment: Impact Report*, KPMG International, Sydney, 27 November 2018.

22 Just Reinvest NSW, 'Justice Reinvestment in Bourke', 2022, https://www.justreinvest.org.au/justice-reinvestment-in-bourke (viewed April 2022).

23 See, for example, Australian Institute of Health and Welfare, 'Literature Review of the Impact of Early Childhood Education and Care on Learning and Development', working paper, cat. no. CWS 53, AIHW, Canberra, 2015.

24 Lawrence J Schweinhart et al., *Lifetime Effects: The High/Scope Perry Preschool Study through Age 40*, High/Scope Press, Ypsilanti, MI, 2005.

25 James J Heckman, 'Skill Formation and the Economics of Investing in Disadvantaged Children', *Science*, vol. 312, no. 5782, June 2006, pp. 1900–2.

26 Relevant evidence can be found in, for example, Marina Sounoglou and Aikaterini Michalopoulou, 'Early Childhood Education Curricula: Human Rights and Citizenship in Early Childhood Education', *Journal of Education and Learning*, vol. 6, no. 2, 2017, pp. 53–68.

27 For a useful discussion of the rights-based approach to early childhood education, see Maria Herczog, 'Rights of the Child and Early Childhood Education and Care in Europe', *European Journal of Education*, vol. 47, no. 4, 2012, pp. 542–55.

28 Australian Institute of Health and Welfare, 'Childcare and Early Childhood Education: Snapshot', AIHW, Canberra, 16 September 2021.

29   See, for example, William Teager, Stacey Fox and Neil Stafford, 'How Australia Can Invest Early and Return More: A New Look at the $15b Cost and Opportunity', Early Intervention Foundation, The Front Project and CoLab at the Telethon Kids Institute, Australia, 2019.

30   This quote is ubiquitous. It can be found, along with key details on the life of Rosa Parks, at the website https://rosaparksfacts.com/rosa-parks-quotes (viewed April 2022).

31   Royal Commission into Aged Care Quality and Safety, *Final Report*, vol. 1, 2021, p. 66.

32   Ibid.

33   Ibid.

34   See Anna Cody and Maria Nawaz, 'UN Slams Australia's Human Rights Record', *The Conversation*, 10 November 2017.

35   The factual information in this section is based on content presented in Australian Institute of Health and Welfare, *Aboriginal and Torres Strait Islander Health Performance Framework 2020: Summary Report*, cat. no. IHPF 2, AIHW, Canberra, 2020.

36   For further discussion of this, see Australian Institute of Health and Welfare, 'Culturally Safe Health Care for Indigenous Australians', AIHW, Canberra, 2020.

37   Australian Institute of Health and Welfare, *Indigenous Health and Wellbeing*, AIHW, Canberra, 2020.

38   See Megan Ann Campbell, Jennifer Hunt, David J Scrimgeour, Maureen Davey and Victoria Jones,

'Contribution of Aboriginal Community-Controlled Health Services to Improving Aboriginal Health: An Evidence Review', *Australian Health Review*, vol. 42, no. 2, 2017, pp. 218–26; Sophia Couzos, 'How to Reform Primary Health Care to Close the Gap', *The Conversation*, 4 April 2016; and Kylie Gwynne and Michelle Lincoln, 'Developing the Rural Health Workforce to Improve Australian Aboriginal and Torres Strait Islander Health Outcomes: A Systematic Review', *Australian Health Review*, vol. 41, no. 2, 2016, pp. 234–8.

39 Paul Karp, 'Marriage Equality Law Passes Australia's Parliament in Landslide Vote', *The Guardian*, 7 December 2017.

40 See, for example, Liam Elphick, 'Marriage Equality Was Momentous, But There Is Still Much to Do to Progress LGBTI+ Rights in Australia', *The Conversation*, 6 March 2019; and Paula Gerber, 'Six Months after Marriage Equality There's Much to Celebrate – and Still Much to Do', *The Conversation*, 3 July 2018.

41 Sean Kelly, 'People and Politics', *The Monthly*, 25 November 2016.

42 Dieter Wolke and Suzet Tanya Lereya, 'Long-Term Effects of Bullying', *Archives of Disease in Childhood*, vol. 100, no. 9, 2015, pp. 879–85.

43 See Ian Rivers, 'The Bullying of Sexual Minorities at School: Its Nature and Long-Term Correlates', *Educational and Child Psychology*, vol. 18, no. 1, 2001,

pp. 32–46; and Jacqueline Ullman, *Free2Be … Yet?: The Second National Study of Australian High School Students Who Identify as Gender and Sexuality Diverse*, Centre for Educational Research, School of Education, Western Sydney University, Penrith, NSW, 2021.

44 Dieter Wolke and Suzet Tanya Lereya, 'Long-Term Effects of Bullying', *Archives of Disease in Childhood*, vol. 100, no. 9, 2015, pp. 879–85.

45 Jacqueline Ullman, *Free2Be … Yet?: The Second National Study of Australian High School Students Who Identify as Gender and Sexuality Diverse*, Centre for Educational Research, School of Education, Western Sydney University, Penrith, NSW, 2021.

46 Ibid.

47 Dieter Wolke and Suzet Tanya Lereya, 'Long-Term Effects of Bullying', *Archives of Disease in Childhood*, vol. 100, no. 9, 2015, pp. 879–85.

48 See, for example, The Diversity Council of Australia, 'Out at Work: From Prejudice to Pride', 13 August 2018.

49 Tania Ferfolja and Jacqueline Ullman, '4 out of 5 Parents Support Teaching Gender and Sexuality Diversity in Australian Schools', *The Conversation*, 15 February 2022.